FROM THE HEART-INSPIRATIONAL POEMS

FROM THE HEART- INSPIRATIONAL POEMS

To Bring You Comfort, Support and a Peace of Mind in Your Time of Need

Michelle Washington

From The Heart Publishing Company
P.O. Box 8244
Albany, NY
12208-0244

Print information available on the last page.

Rev. date: 09/30/2022

To order additional copies of this book, contact:
Xlibris
844-714-8691
www.Xlibris.com
Orders@Xlibris.com
535660

CONTENTS

Section 3

Section 4

Section 5

Section 6

Section 7

~Going Home Celebration~

Acknowledgements

I give all the glory and honor to God who is my foundation. I thank Him for being the wind beneath my wings and for never leaving me nor forsaken me. Without Him, I wouldn't exist and because of Him, I shall not perish.

I dedicate this book to my mother, the late Charlie Mae Everett, who has always instilled in her children the incredible gift of the fruit of the spirit and has taught us to value what we believe in and to never lose focus of our *Salvation. Jesus Christ.* The legacy that my mom left behind, her commitment, passion and love for *Jesus Christ*, her family and the community, speaks for itself. No one will ever forget Mrs. Charlie Mae. Mom your living has not been in vain. God has called you home for His word stands to say; good job my good and faithful servant, Charlie Mae, job well done. We love you!

To my family: Chevis, Chanel, Demetris, Tiffany, Brian, Diemere, JW, Ameian, Taezi, Myaira, Davian, Ikei, Matthew, Linda, Clarice, Maxcine, Lesia, and to all of my uncles, aunts, nephews, and nieces, I love you and I thank God for this unity. I want to especially thank my sister Maxcine for her time, guidance and support while pushing me to complete my work. Love you all.

My godchildren: Sean, Rashiem, Nehemiah, Imani, Sandar, Meosha, Efua, Marquis, Queyanna and Dominique. I thank God for the blessed privilege of being your godmother.

To all of my children in the community who look up to me as mom or auntie, remember, I will always be there for you.

My dear friends Pearl and Gina thank you for being a part of my life and for your dedicated friendship.

My sister in Christ and prayer partner, Sis. Debra Rambus, thank you for being a tremendous support in my life. You are truly a blessing.

Pastors Donald and Apostle Rose Stuart, I thank God for you, you have been a blessing in my life. Thank you for allowing me to sit under and serve in leadership. A ministry that functions according to the Lords mandates and under the guidance of the Holy Spirit. If anybody knows, you do, that Jesus Christ is worthy to be praised!

Thanks to all for supporting me and believing in me. God bless you. Love to all.

Introduction

Writing poetry has always been a part of my life. It's a part of healing. Through these inspirational poems I pray that they will bring you strength when you are weak, encourage you when discouraged, and comfort you when you feel lonely. Most of all, I hope they bring peace and balance where hearts are separated.

SECTION 1

Your rights

You have the right to hear the gospel.
Once you have heard the gospel,
everything you say and do from this point on
will be judged through the eyes of God.

You have the right to receive eternal life
through Jesus Christ, as He becomes your personal savior.
If you choose not to receive Jesus Christ as your personal savior,
a personal death sentence will be appointed for you by Satan.

Satan will give you the desire of his heart, death,
destruction and eternity in hell!

Judgment day is soon approaching.
Have your name added to the book of life.
Follow the Lords commandments.
Love one another as Jesus Christ loves you.

Spend eternity in heaven
with perfect peace and everlasting praise
with our redeemer, Jesus Christ our Lord.

Amen.

The Gift of Life

My Lord, you thought enough of me to bless me with the gift of life!

You had plans for me to conquer and plans for me to succeed.
I thank you for this gift of life!
I promise that I will always praise you without a doubt,
with all the gifts, talents and joy that you have instilled in me.

The road that you traveled to free me from sin,
gave me the will to live and to look forward to
being with you until the eternal end!

My Lord, I thank you for this gift of life!
I thank for your amazing grace oh! How sweet the sound!

Your grace will shine through me for other's to see
how thankful we should be.

Amen.

A smile

A smile is worth a million words.
It brings forth happiness and joy.

A smile shows that there is hope.

A smile brings forth cheer, peace and abundant love.

A smile shows signs of caring, comfort and understanding.

A smile can mend a broken heart. What an awesome gift to share!

A smile sends forth messages and answers that you've prayed for.

A smile shows signs of healing, we know that it's good for the soul.

A smile will win you friends, one's that you will adore.

A smile shows signs of grace and wisdom that you will enjoy.

A smile can last a lifetime. What more could you ask for?

Amen.

A treasured friend

We share dreams and we share secrets.

We share laughter and we share tears.

We share joy and we share sorrow.

But most of all, we share the same desire,

a treasured friend, Jesus Christ our Lord.

Amen.

Rise

Until we rise we will never make a difference.

Until we rise things will never change.

Until we rise we will never come together.

*   *   *

When we rise we can come together and accomplish much.
When we rise we can succeed at what we set forth to achieve.
When we rise we can deliver by making a difference in the lives of those in need.

Amen.

Lord, let the presence of your light shine through me

Let the reflection of your mirror touch everyone that I come in contact with.

Use me, Oh Lord, as your vessel to show other's that there is hope.

Through me, let the miracle of your touch comfort those in need.

Through my eyes, let your light shine on those living in darkness so that they can see that there is a way out.

Let my feet lead those to your glory, for you said that you have paved the way.

Lord, let my arms extend to those near and afar so that they won't feel that they're all alone.

Let my heart remain full of love and compassion for those who didn't know that you were the only way, for when they gain the knowledge of your Glory, it will save them in everyway.

Let my words flow with harmony for those who need to hear your word day after day.

Let my ears become spiritual listeners to those who may just need someone to talk too.

Let my mind stay focused on fulfilling the mission that you have called me to do and that is to lead others to Salvation. What a perfect gift to have eternal life with you!

Lord, use every breath in my body at your will.
For it was you who gave me the breath of life and for that I say, Halleluiah!

Amen.

Inventory Prayer

Dear Heavenly Father, I thank you for blessing me with the gift of life. I thank you for your everlasting love and your word, which will stand forever. I thank you for the gifts and talents that you have blessed me with. I thank you for your Son, Jesus Christ, whom you sent to set me free.

I ask that you take inventory over my life and correct any mistakes and wrong doings for which I surely repent. speak to my mind, Oh Lord, when the enemy tries to trap me. Father, purify my life with your Holy Spirit. Create me a pure heart for I know that the closest gift that I can give to you is my heart.

Father, teach me to be a better steward over my household and my finances. Strengthen me when the pressure gets rough. If you see me stray, I ask you to turn me around and plant my feet back on solid ground.

Father, show me the road that will lead me to fulfill the mission and purpose that you have ordained for my life.

Help me to be a better parent and positive role model for my children. If my children rebel against me, I ask you to step in and bridge the gap.

Father, I ask that you would put people in my life that would be a help to me in my time of need. I pray that when the time comes for me to depart from this world that I would have left a legacy that would live on, and that I would have touched the lives of many by making a difference.

Father, I ask all these things in the name of your only begotten Son Jesus Christ, who will forever and ever reign over my life.

Amen.

Mother, I thank you

Mother, you are the fruit of the earth,

the maker of ones affection,

the gentleness of ones nature,

the softness of ones touch,

the treasure to ones heart,

the comfort of ones speech,

the choice of ones love.

From the beginning you were chosen as the nurturer to deliver fruit from your womb, the birth of God's inheritance, His children. Through all that I may have put you through, you have always said that I was worth it.

For this, Mother, I thank you.

Your Destiny

Your attitude will reflect your outcome.

Your determination will keep you motivated.

Your goals will challenge you to stay focused,

and will lead you in the right direction.

As you travel towards your destiny,

you will prevail.

Change

Seasons change to show the beauty of God's creation.

People change to become one season, in one body, in one Spirit, and on

One accord, to show the manifestation of one mind, in one Christ, (Jesus)!

Amen.

A Virtuous Woman

She is a woman who loves and fears the Lord with all her heart.

She wears her crown with dignity and integrity.

She never neglects her responsibilities.

Her children arise and call her blessed.

She uses wisdom in everything she does.

She shows compassion and blesses those in need.

She takes pride in her work.

She uses her gifts and talent's to glorify the Lord.

She values and provides for her family.

She is a woman of decency and order.

She's looked up to with much respect.

She walks by faith.

Her light shines wherever she goes.

She is a servant that the Lord will look to and will surely say,

"good job, my good and faithful servant, job well done."

Amen.

Spread your wings and fly

You are a beautiful creature in the sight of God.

God made you just the way you are.

When you spread your wings, you can always fly high.

You fly towards the mountains, you fly towards the sky.

God made you so that you can fly above,

all the hurt and pain.

Don't altar yourself for someone else's temptation.

Any unacceptable changes they will look at you from afar.

You will see that this isn't who you are.

God doesn't make mistakes in what he creates.

Go back to who God created before it's too late.

Spread your wings and fly!

Amen.

Cherished memories

Whenever I think of you, I feel lonely and sad.

As I'm reminded of you, the tears start to flow

I cry openly, I cry silently

they are tears of missing you and tears of joy.

Joy for the thoughts when I think of the wonderful times we shared together.

Tears for the thoughts when I'm missing your presence because you are know longer around.

I cherish the times that we shared together, moments so precious, rewarding and great.

Those are the times that will get me through tomorrow, while I make it through today.

Amen.

Words of Encouragement

I *can*

I *will*

I'll try

I believe

I'll succeed

I'll achieve

I'll survive

We can come together

We can come together
Together as one
To fight for our children
God's chosen one's

We are living in times
Where violence is on the rise
Let's not sit around and watch
Like we don't care

For our children are dying
At the hands of one another
We can stop the violence
If we come together as one
We must teach them to love
And not hate each other for gain
And to stop ending their lives this way

For our children are our future
That's why God placed them in our lives
To protect and guide them
And to lead them in His word

Mother's are weeping
While fathers have gone astray
We must be there for our children
For this is God's way

We can come together
Together as one
To fight for our children
God's chosen one's

We have the foundation
God's Holy ground
As a community—we can conquer all

We can come together
Together as one
To fight for our children
God's chosen one's

It takes you and I to give
Our children a chance in life
We know prayer can change things
Let's teach them how to pray

For our children are dying
At the hands of one another
Let's teach them to walk away
From situations—that will end their lives this way
If we love our children, let's show them that we care

We can come together, together as one.

SECTION 2

Faith

F—is for the **Fulfillment** of the purpose that God has for your life.

A—is for the **Assurance** that the Lord will lead you along the way.

I—is for the **Image** of who we represent, our creator, God.

T—is for the **Testimonies**, which we share of His grace and mercy that He provides in our lives everyday.

H—is for standing by His Holy Word as we shout **Hallelujah** and Praise His Holy Name.

Amen.

A Mother's Prayer

Dear Heavenly Father, I thank you for the blessings that only you could give. I thank you for blessing my womb to carry such a rewarding gift, the creation of life! I pray that my children will grow up and take with them the biblical principles they were taught, and not turn to the ways of the world.

I pray that my children will use wisdom in everything they do, by seeking you first. Lord, I pray for you to give me strength to walk through this journey of being a parent. I pray for patience, guidance, wisdom and understanding.

Lord, I know that there is evidence of peer pressure facing my children, such as gangs, violence, drugs, death and disobedience. Father, I pray that my children will lose sight of the flesh and open up their eyes to the spirit and realize that no weapon formed against them shall prosper and understand that the battle is not theirs.

I pray that my children realize that they shouldn't wrestle against the flesh and blood, against principles, against powers, against rulers of darkness of the world, against spiritual wickedness in high places.

I pray for them to receive the blessings and purpose that you've written for their life, and know that you are their hope, peace, direction and Jehovah Jireh, our provider. I pray that my children will always hold on to you and never, ever, lose sight of their salvation to eternal life!

Amen.

Do you hear me now?

I've been crucified and convicted, by those that I thought loved and cared about me.

It seems like my life is falling apart and the shattered pieces are too heavy for me to bear.

My children have gone astray. They no longer listen to instruction; they say,

that they have already heard.

My marriage is failing; the vows of the promises and commitments have not been fulfilled.

The responsibilities are not being shared.

My finances have crumbled as I have borrowed my way to closed doors.

The bill collectors are calling. I have to worry about being left in the dark,

because my cash flow is no more.

I have been left to carry all the burdens and the weight, with no changes nor gain.

My health is failing, the stress and anxiety is over whelming, and does anybody really care?

Do you hear me now?

My house is tumbling down and many repairs still remain.

My peace of mind had been lost and I felt that it would never be found.

I have no time to myself because my time has always been there for all.

My brothers, my sisters, if you say that you don't understand what I am going through,

I would like to take this opportunity, to invite you to walk in my shoes.

Do you hear me now?

There is this voice in my head that keeps telling me there is hope

and to hold on to my faith because the Lord is no joke!

I said to the Lord, that the people have turned there back on me and asked how could this be true?

Lord, because of my giving I have been misunderstood.

Lord, I ask you now, Oh Lord, what must I do?

You said, my child, I want you too understand, in my sight, you have been a faithful servant

and your labor hasn't been in vain.

I Am your Great Master, so lets follow my plan, and you can rest assure that my word still stands.

If you are heavy laden, in which you have surely been, come and seek me, The Great, I Am!

What you have been going through, was only a test,

now you can see why it is so important for you to communicate with me.

The Beginning and the End!

Man may toss you to the curb, but I want you to know that I Am always
a man of my word.

So, no matter what you go through, we are never apart.
Those that are quick to judge you,

let them cast the first stone.

Pray for those that have persecuted and have failed you that they sin no more.

Cry no more, my servant. I want your life to be full of my joy.

Do you hear me now?

Amen.

My little butterfly!

My little butterfly you are so precious, gentle and sweet!

My little butterfly you are my blessing and my wonderful gift of joy.

My little butterfly your smiles bring me hope and bring me cheer.

My little butterfly, if you fall because your wings failed to fly, I will be
there to lift you up.

My little butterfly I will help make your dreams come true.

My little butterfly always remember that I love you.

What A Man

Have you ever wondered about the destiny of your soul and who is in control? Have you ever wondered who has freed you of your sins and makes promises that are true to His everlasting word?

"What A Man," that would give up His life for you, give you dominion over the earth, give you the power to ask for anything in His name and you receive it.

"What A Man," that has the ability to write your name in the book of life and travel with you throughout your gift of eternal life!

"What A Man," that by calling on His name, will make you tremble!

"What A Man," who is full of purpose and direction. Speaks words into existence, creates with the wave of His hand and breathes life into the vessels of the earth. "Jesus Christ, my Lord, "What A Man'!

Amen.

A Creative Mind

A creative mind will take you far.

A creative mind will lead you in the direction that you want to go.

A creative mind will expose the gifts and talents that you were blessed with.

A creative mind will block out the spirit of fear, doubt, intimidation, jealousy, rejection, obstacles and procrastination.

A creative mind will prove that you are more than a conqueror, because you will always know who's image you were created in.

A creative mind will bring you prosperity and wealth.

A creative mind will allow you to step out on faith and will reveal your success.

A creative mind will prove that you are unique.

A creative mind will show the world that you are a believer of Jesus Christ and trust in Him to develop what He has instilled within you.

A creative mind will always deliver by allowing the Lord to guide you, and not the ways of the world to mislead you.

Amen.

A faithful servant

A faithful servant is one who with honor, submits to following the will of the Lord.

A faithful servant is one who humbly, submits to their leaders and completes whatever tasks delegated for them to do.

A faithful servant will always seek the kingdom of God.

A faithful servant will go to the aid of others when there is a need.

A faithful servant will pray without ceasing.

A faithful servant will walk by faith and not by sight.

A faithful servant is one who does good deeds from their heart.

A faithful servant is one who willfully gives their tithes and offerings without mumbling or grudging.

A faithful servant is one who girdles their tongue and doesn't let outside influences pull them astray.

A faithful servant always forgives.

A faithful servant is one who willfully follows the
Mission & Vision of their church.

A faithful servant is wise and wins souls to Christ.

A faithful servant will surely get their name added to the book of life.

A faithful servant is one who shows the love of Jesus Christ from within.

A faithful servant is one that the Lord, will look too and say, good job
my good and faithful servant, job well done.

Amen.

Giving all thanks to my God

I thank God for creating me.

I thank God for waking me up this morning.

I thank God for guiding me along the way.

I thank God for allowing me to praise Him another day.

I thank God for the smiles that came along the way.

I thank God for all the joy He has placed in my life.

I thank God for never leaving me or forsaking me.

I thank God for being in my life in everyway.

Amen.

Together

Together we can conquer all, step over fear

and build bridges over troubled waters.

Together we can close our minds on division, and create new beginnings.

Together we can share our past an plan for our future.

Together we can pray, fast and heal.

Together we can open doors for our children, provide them with
opportunity, direction and vision.

Together we can help our children achieve their goals, develop their plans,
personalize their dreams, show them how to gather their inheritance and
how to sow their seed in good ground.

Together we can teach our children how to read and write, how to
become productive young men and women of society.

Together we can deliver.

God's blessings for you

Let your days be sunny
with the blessings sent from above.
For God made today and tomorrow
So you could be filled with His unconditional love.

Amen.

Lord take over my life

Lord, I pray that you strengthen my mind so that your word may be manifested in my life and in the lives of those I come in contact with. So, they too may receive the beautiful blessings contained by your unconditional love.

Lord, I thank you for bridging the gap with your presence in times when I feel lonely, depressed or even feel like giving up.

I know all things work together for the good of those who love you. Lord, it's because of you that I shall not be tricked, fooled, misguided or robbed of my blessings, salvation or peace by any of satan's tasks.

Lord, take over my life, for with you I am secured.

Amen.

The greatest moments in a parent's life

The birth of their children

Their children's relationship with God.

Their children graduating from high school and college.

Their children becoming a productive member of society.

Amen.

SECTION 3

My sister's look where the Lord has brought us from

Remembering back in your past, when you thought there was no way out!
Overcome with fear and destruction.
Always feeling left with doubt.

Surrounded by those spirits of lust, addictions and mistrust,
filled with emptiness inside.

Your mind being controlled by demons that only offered you death, grief and pain.
Not knowing that you had choices that could help you gain.

Because of your Insecurities above and beyond your control
you found you're surrounded by your biggest fear, "Failure".

You were depending on the world to bring you through, finding yourself
filled with false hopes and promises that never brought you change,
homeless, living on the streets, with no shelter insight.

Holding on to those words of discouragement,
always told that you wouldn't amount to
anything. You never tried because you thought you had nothing to gain.

Confused in your spirit about your existence and how you would prevail.
Not knowing that you have a purpose in life.

Sitting there all alone thinking that there was no relief in sight.
Suddenly! There was a check in your spirit that said enough my
child it's time to move on!
A whisper in your ear telling you to surrender and call the name of the
Great I Am!
"Jesus Christ".

He is the one who brought you out of darkness and directed you into the light.
He filled you with hope, peace, determination and the will to live and not die.
He assured you that you are somebody because he made you in his image.
You know longer have to suffer, because it was he who bore your pain.

You are prosperous my sister's! Full of wisdom, knowledge and grace, born again and filled with the Holly Spirit which will take you to the promise land.

Focus on the Glory of Salvation, for it's the King that will help you to survive.
He will never leave nor forsake you, for he is the only way.

Focus on your future and you will never return to your past.
When you find yourself going through the eye of the storm call on Jesus to pull you out!

While faith of a mustard seed could move mountains along the way, believe in yourself and your accomplishments and all that you can achieve.
Your faith in Jesus Christ will guide you along the way.

P.U.S.H! My sister's P.U.S.H! It's your prayers that will bring you through.
My sister's, stand and shout "Hallelujah" give glory and honor to whom it's due.

AMEN.

His touch

He touched my mind

He touched my heart

He touched my spirit

He touched my soul

He touched my life and He made me whole.

Amen.

Mercy

Father, I thank you for your mercy

it's by your grace that I make it through

I thank you for your time and commitment

and for your patience, I thank you too.

Amen.

Don't take away my vision

Don't steal my peace, comfort and joy.

Don't shatter my goals, accomplishments and pride.

Don't bury my dreams, hopes and desires.

Don't take away my vision,

allow me to fly!

Amen.

My Perfect Peace

When my spirit is not resting
my soul cries out with pain
feeling untouched, by that perfect peace.

It's when the presence of the enemy is hanging around my path
not leaving me room to walk a straight line, only broken steps to
stumble and fall.

It's time for me to take a stand as I know; I have a choice and the upper hand.

A choice to find my perfect peace so, that I could walk with thee.
When I walk with thee, my spirit will find rest
as my soul cries out with joy!

I pray for that perfect peace to always abide in me.

Amen.

Lord direct my path

There were many roads that were open for me to follow,
many directions for me to go, many sights for me to see and many
decisions I had to make.

I often got confused, whether it was because of the lack of knowledge,
which I failed to gain, lack of wisdom, which I failed to receive, or my
instincts, which I haven't yet learned.

I often made the wrong choices and received misguided information.
Lord, was it because I was looking for hope from the world and not from
your will?
Was my vision impaired because I took my eyes off of the sparrow?
Did my dreams die because I didn't seek your kingdom first?
Did you not hear my cries because it was not your shoulder that I was
leaning on?

My Lord, I apologize for being disobedient and not looking towards you, my future my eternal life! When I look back at all that I tried to accomplish and at how often I tried to succeed, all to realize that my failures came because I didn't seek you as my guide.

Lord direct my path.

Amen.

My true friend

When I am weak you give me strength.

When I am down you lift me up.

When I frown you make me smile.

When I cry you wipe away my tears.

When I am lost you always find me.

When I am sad you make me laugh.

When I need a friend you are always there.

"Thank you, **Jesus Christ**, my true friend".

Amen.

Don't give up

It's not about how you fall, but how you get back up.

It's not about you failing, but what steps you will take to succeed.

It's not about your nightmares, but your hopes and
dreams you hold for today.

It's not about what others will think of you, but what you think of yourself.

It's not about winning the race, but the attempt you took to make it to
the finish line.

It's not about your set backs, but your effort you made to move forward.

It's the challenge you face today that will get you through tomorrow.

Receive

You can't teach what you don't know.

You can't share what you don't have.

You can't give what you haven't received.

You can't receive what's for you, if you don't let go of what's not.

The inner voice

When I feel like I am about to lose my mind and want to give up, the
inner voice speaks to me and says, "don't worry it's going to be okay,
allow me to take over your thoughts and the joy of receiving me will
become your strength".

When I feel like I am all alone and that there is no one to talk too, or
help me in my time of need, the inner voice speaks to me and says,
"don't worry it's going to be okay, seek me first, talk to me. I'll be your
friend and I'll supply all of your needs.

When I 'm feeling pressured, tired and weary, the inner voice speaks to me and says, "don't worry it's going to be okay, come unto me when you labor and are heavy laden and I will give you rest.

When I feel like the odds are against me, the world is against me, or when I don't have confidence in myself, the inner voice speaks to me and says, "don't worry it's going to be okay, because I am for you no one can be against you.
Confide in me, I am above all. "I will never leave you nor forsake you".

When the road is rocky and I stumble and fall, the inner voice speaks to me and says, "don't worry it's going to be okay, when you fall I will pick you up, turn you around and plant your feet back on solid ground.

The inner voice is "**Jesus Christ**".

His promise is to be with me until the end of time.

Amen.

No more sin

I was lost and bound in a world of sin.
I turned in every direction there within.
It was that glorious day that I invited Jesus into my life
Halleluiah! I was never the same again!

What I am trying to say to you,
don't let other's negativity influence you.
Life isn't something you just through away.
It's a gift the Lord has blessed you with.

I thought I was doing the right things in life,
until one day, my life was set out on the line.
It was then that I knew I didn't fit in,
the crowd just stood around and watched
as the gang tried to do me in.

An angel stood over me and whispered in my ear,
call on Jesus, and you will be sure to win.
It was that time I called on Him.
Halleluiah! I was never the same again!

Try and make the best of your life.
If you are unsure as to what you should do,
call on Jesus, and you will be sure to win.
Halleluiah! I will never be the same again!

Once I found salvation in Jesus Christ,
I finally felt good about my life.
I didn't know that this was all it took,
was to invite Jesus Christ into my life.
Jesus is the one, I can surely say,
will never turn His back on you, in anyway.

I felt low and cold when I was living in sin.
I am glad I got the opportunity to change my life within.
Halleluiah! I will never be the same again! No more sin!

Amen.

Positive Choices

Be an Individual

Keep yourself safe

Use your own mind

"DON'T BE A FOLLOWER OF GANGS"

GATHERING
AMONGST
NEGATIVE
GUIDANCE

SECTION 4

Believe in yourself

If you dream it, make it come true.

If it's your goal, accomplish it.

If you have a mission, follow it.

If it is for you, except it.

When you believe in yourself you can make things happen.
Don't let fear step in the way to stop you from succeeding in life.

A Teacher's Prayer

Dear Lord, I thank you for providing me with the opportunity to teach.
I am grateful for being able to give back to society, what was given to
me, an education.

I pray that the student's that sit under my instruction will have an open
mind to learn, an attentive ear to listen, a passionate heart to receive and
a Godly spirit to overcome any obstacles or fears they may face.

I pray that the knowledge that my student's receive will lead them
through their journey to succeed by accomplishing their dreams, desires
and goals. I pray that my student's will come back as productive
members of society and contribute to other's success.

Amen.

A Dose of Reality

God

Prevention

Perfection

Commitment

Mom, I love you

Mom, I felt it was to soon for you to leave me. But God felt a need to call you home. I hadn't prepared myself for your departure: but I now realize that you had to move on.

I will always remember your smile, your laughter and your fragrance, what a pleasant scent!
Your presence and our memories will continually live in my heart.

Mom, the most rewarding experience, that I have ever had was your introducing me to Jesus Christ.
Oh! I've sure been blessed.

I am glad that God chose you to be my mother. I find that I inherited a lot of your ways, but that's ok because it's all-good in everyway.

Knowing God and believing in His promises, we will see each other again. Yes, the opportunity will arise for me to tell you how much I love you again!
Even though I miss your touch and those encouraging words that you often gave, I am glad that you're with Jesus, for there is no better place.

Amen.

Time out

How often do you feel like giving up? Things aren't as easy as they seem to be. Everyone thinks that you have it all under control. What they don't know is the pain you are feeling deep inside. Always under stress, pressure and worrying all the time.

The responsibilities are over whelming. Oh! Where is time out? When everyone salutes you for all your efforts, you don't have the Energy to salute back. Sometimes it feels like you are taking on a whole army and all you have to fight back with is a toothpick. It will break every time.

You are responsible for so many minds and decisions day after day. Where is your support, someone you can talk too and lend you a hand in your time of need? You find yourself crying more than smiling.

You find yourself stuck in a time frame. So, therefore you run out of time for yourself. If you don't find time for yourself, time will continue to find you for everyone else.

My Covenant is with you

How are you? I haven't heard from you in a while. What 's going on? Who have you been hanging out with lately that has been taking up all of your time?

Did you forget who I am? I will introduce myself to you again. I am Jesus Christ. I created you; I gave you life, my child. I love you. I am a very jealous person. I miss your praises! I have always given you everything that you ever asked for.

Come back home to me and dwell in my presence. I will always keep my promise to you. I will never leave you nor forsake you.

It saddens me when my children turn there back on me. I am the one who was sacrificed at Calvary, so that you could have eternal life? I'm the one who was nailed to the cross; with stakes in my hands and feet. It was I who was beaten beyond recognition. I bore your strips on by back, and the crown of thorns in my head. It was I who was pierced in the side and as the blood came streaming down, it was you who I was thinking of. I did this to protect you, my child, so that you wouldn't have to suffer. It was my blood, which washed away your sins.

It's you who I love. I died for you, my child, and rose from the dead to be with you forever. It is the world that will keep you in bondage, but only I who can set you free.

I am here sitting at the right hand of Our Father, interceding for you. Come out of darkness and follow the light. Repent and come back to me. My Covenant is with you, always. My child. I love you.

Jesus

Patience

Like lilies on the vine waiting patiently to bloom, giving off it's sweet scents and pleasant aromas.

Watching the thunder & lighting on a cloudy day while the earth is waiting patiently to receive the rain.

Preparing for destiny while rejoicing in my spirit, patiently waiting for the mission that God has called me to do.

"Thank you Lord"

What a wonderful time that will be. I will be singing with harmony while the strings flow from the harp.

Listening to the whistles from the trees and watching the praises from the leaves.

Hearing the sounds of the ocean waves, patiently waiting with gratitude of welcome to receive.

Oh! How patient shall I be, through my patients, I will graciously receive.

Waiting patiently is all I need; patience will deliver "indeed".

Amen.

A Father's Prayer

Dear Heavenly Father, I thank you for all that you've done in my life. Heavenly Father, I thank you for the opportunity of allowing me to be the priest over my household.

Heavenly Father, I thank you for my family. I pray that you protect them from harm and danger. My prayer is that my household will never lose focus of their salvation, for you are our rock, our fortress and deliverer.

My prayer is that my children will look up to me as a positive role model in their life. When my children are away from home my prayer is that they will use wisdom in everything they do, and value the biblical principles, which they were taught.

My prayer is that my children will grow up to be productive men and woman of society and that your light will continue to shine through them.

Amen.

All is Real

All is real, because it is He who heals.

All is real, because it is He who frees.

All is real, because it is He who cares.

All is real, because it is He who loves.

All is real, because it is He who made the sacrifice.

All is real, because it is he who showed Himself approved.

All is real, because it is He who provides.

All is real, because it is He who delivers.

All is real, because it is He who sees all.

All is real, because it is He who creates.

All is real, because it is He who anoints.

All is real, because it is He who has the power.

All is real, because it is He who made the difference.

All is real, because it is He who is the cause.

All is real, because it is He who is real.

All is real, because if you only believe, you will realize that reality is real and that reality is "JESUS CHRIST".

Amen.

God's chosen

Father, I pray for my shepherd's

as they continue to lead your way.

I will seek your guidance,

as I am filled with your word day after day.

Anoint them with your glory,

as they were chosen to represent you from above.

Father, I thank you for your chosen one's,

as they manifest their love.

Amen.

Reach me before you approach me

If you "approach" me before you try to reach me, you may wind up losing me.

If you "reach" me before you approach me, you may surely find me.

Your position doesn't empress me, though your title states who you are.

The words you speak from your mouth can bring me closer, or they can surely turn me away.

Your attitude in your approach is a reflection of how you choose to greet.

So, maybe that's a chance you shouldn't take, until your attitude is straight.

If you show me some compassion, my heart will open to receive you without a debate.

If you flaunt your position, my heart will close, trust me, your wasting your time with someone who knows.

So, turn your attitude around, which is all it takes.

Reach then approach, it will guarantee a rebate.

Amen.

Thank you Lord for your Grace

I know that I am only a child and I must continue to grow.
Knowing that I have you by my side things will not be as hard as I thought.

Your plans for my life and the things that you have called me to do are
an easy pattern to follow, full of insight and truth.

It's through you that I know I can conquer the world, and make all my
dreams come true.

While there is breath in my body. I will prepare others for your return.

They will learn of you through your Gospel and hunger for your word
day after day.

It's your will for me to make it to the promise land and that
I will surely do.

Thank you Lord for creating me.

I do give Glory and honor to you.

Amen.

Spoiled

You haven't been spoiled until

you have been spoiled by the Holy Spirit.

Amen.

SECTION 5

What is life

Life is a plan of God's will
Developed in the womb
Begins with your first breath
Full of emotions & feelings

Dreams & visions
Harmony, hope and peace
Giving & receiving
Loving and being loved
Caring and sharing
Opportunity and positions
Awareness and temptation

Joy and desire
Hugs and kisses
Hope and acceptance
Comfort and laughter
Choices and decisions
Aspiration and trust
Talent's and gifts

Beautiful, precious and sweet
Family and friends
Commitment and faithfulness
Awesome and breathtaking
Goals and success
Mission and purpose
Life is worthwhile

Most of all life can be eternal and everlasting
through, Jesus Christ our Lord.

Thank you and God bless you.

Amen.

A Gift

A gift is something you receive,

you treasure, value, appreciate, cherish

and protect it.

It's something that you can hold on

to for a lifetime.

I am blessed by being a blessing to you

You will never know what I'm blessed with if you keep rejecting my willingness.

When I bring you ideas, you just toss them aside.

When I bring you suggestions, you can never agree.

When I bring you correction you look at me and say, this is not your calling, you just turn away.

When I bring you commitment your rejection states to say, when I need you, I will call you, but for now just stay away!

Knowledge

Knowledge is power, without it you are weak.

Knowledge brings forth awareness.

Knowledge brings forth correction.

Knowledge brings forth hope.

Knowledge brings forth change.

Obtain it!
Believe in it!
Share it!

Don't get caught without it.

Let's Celebrate the Birth of Christ

"Christmas"

The true meaning of Christmas in not about the presents under the tree.
It's about the glorious gift of a Baby Boy so Precious, Rewarding and
Great. It's about The Star in the East that shined over the stable of the
one and only lying in the Manger wrapped in swaddling cloth.

It's about the beginning of a miracle and the Truth that came to save us
and free us of our sins. It's about the true provider our Savior, the
everlasting, The Messiah, the beginning of life.
The Great I Am.

It's a time for Celebration, Hope, Peace and Amazing Grace. It's a time
for Laughter, Rejoicing, Healing and Thanksgiving.
It's a time of Knowledge, Wisdom and Understanding, a time of
Appreciation, a time to seek the Kingdom of God.
It's a time for Praise and Worship and shout Halleluiah!

Be like the wise men that brought to Him *Gold, Frankincense and Myrrh.*
Let's Celebrate the Birth of the "King" our Landmark and Eternal Life
for all who believe!
Oh! Come let us adore Him.
Amen.

If I could turn back the hands of time

If I could turn back the hands of time,
the first person that I would have wanted to meet is the person that I
know now.
"Jesus Christ".
I wouldn't have had to search so long and hard to find a true friend.

When I met "Jesus", I met someone who I could rely on,
will never turn His back on me,
will never slander me, has my back when others try to cut me down,
intercedes to the Father on my behalf, someone I could talk to and will
guide me in the right direction, someone I can trust, picks me up when I fall,
understands my praise, is not ashamed of the gospel, is always honest with me,
will always tell me the truth, has my best interest at heart,
and promised to never leave me nor forsake me.

Thank you, *Jesus.*

Amen.

Putting your priorities in order

Faith

Family

Business

Recreation

Through it all

Through this life you past but once.

Through your trials you may travel many.

Through your faith doubt may come.

Through your winnings confusion may claim your victory.

Through your opportunities fear may hold you back.

Through your happiness sorrow may rob you of your peace.
Through it all you may be challenged, whether physically, emotionally
or spiritually.

Through it all if you allow Jesus Christ to lead you, you will come out victorious.

Amen.

A Mother's Love

A Mother is someone who God has blessed to give birth, someone who
nurtures her children.

A Mother is someone who prays over her children day and night, someone
who is always there when you need her.

A Mother is someone who keeps peace in the family, someone who is always
there to wipe away your tears.

A Mother is someone who helps plan your social events, and adds that loving touch.

A Mother is someone who is there to watch over you as you grow, someone who will always cheer you on, someone who will always offer you words of encouragement.

A Mother is someone who will go that extra mile to push you to accomplish your goals, someone who will go without in order that her children will be provided for.

A Mother is someone who will keep a smile on your face, someone who you can always come home to.

A Mother is someone who will guide you in making those complicated decisions, someone who holds the family together.

A Mother is someone who will boost you up and lift your spirit!

A Mother is someone who teaches her children right from wrong, someone who supports you when you take that very first step.

A Mother is someone who's there when you get that first tooth and when you say your first word, someone who is there to mend that broken heart, always knowing the right words to say.

A Mother is someone who keeps her promises, someone you can call a true friend.

A Mother is someone who raises her children with Godly principles, someone who comes to the aide of her children when needed.

A Mother is someone who has that "good home cooked meal waiting for you along with those mouth watering deserts" nobody cooks like Mom!

A Mother is someone who always shows her love for her children, genuinely from her heart.

Amen.

Holy Ghost

Watch your back,
because every ghost isn't holy.

Amen.

SECTION 6

I 'm still a child

Don't rob me of my childhood; I don't want to grow up too fast because I might get lost.

When you see me going in the wrong direction, don't scold me; just guide me in the way I should go.

I 'm going to make mistakes, don't criticize me. Let me know it's ok because, it's all a part of learning and encourage me to do better.

Allow me the opportunity to make my own decisions, I can be right; let me show you by giving me a chance.

When I'm feeling sad and can't control my tears, don't push me away, give me a hug, comfort is good for the soul.

I know sometimes you may be busy and if I get in your way it's because, I want your attention, don't get angry with me. I just love being around you.

I know you get frustrated with me when I don't finish my homework or clean my room. sometimes I just may not understand what I'm suppose to do. Don't yell at me or hit me, use that energy to teach me. Learning does start at home.

Don't call me those hurting words like stupid, ignorant, and dumb or tell me that I will never amount to anything. Just remember that I'm a part of you.

When I grow up, I will look back at all my accomplishments and it will be to you whom I will say thank you.

"I love you" your child.

A word for the youth

Put God first in your life and allow Him to direct your path.
Become a productive part of society.
Give your tithes and offerings faithfully.
Be a positive leader and role model.
Do not let negative influences overcome you.

Honor and obey your parents.
Reframe from using drugs and alcohol.
Respect other's property and feelings.
Walk in the spirit of excellence and hold true to your faith.
Pray without ceasing.

Don't let your mind become the devil's playground.
Be wise and win souls to Jesus Christ.
Spend quantity and quality time with your siblings.
Stay focused and complete your education.
Follow your dreams and set goals.

Use wisdom in everything that you do, by seeking God first.
Read your bible daily to show yourself approved unto God.
Keep a Godly attitude.
Appreciate life and everything that it has to offer you.
Don't join gangs; they are misleading.
Fear God and keep His commandments.

Remember, "Jesus Christ is Lord over your life".
For you were bought at a price; therefore glorify God in your body and in
your spirit, which are God's. 1 Corinthians 6:20.
Amen.

My dear love one

The time has come for us to make amends and to put the past behind us.

I am genuinely sorry for anything that I may have done to offend or hurt you.

It's time to blossom new beginnings. It's time to forgive and to let our bond as a family grow.

It was God's plan and purpose when He placed us together, not as enemies, but as a loving family to remain unified and joined together as one in Jesus Christ.

To always be there for one another for better or worse and to provide each other with extended arms of comfort, love, reunions and many hugs.

We must always maintain that connection. There is no better time to ask for forgiveness then at this very moment.
I pray in the name of Jesus, that you would receive this blessing with an open heart.

I Love you.

Unity

As a team, we can unite.
As a community, we can rebuild.
With our faith, we are strong, powerful and bold.
Because of what we proclaim and have endured,
nothing, but nothing, can stop us from accomplishing and achieving,
whatever task set before us.

Dad, I forgive you

Dad, we never made memories together so we can't focus on the past. If you had existed in my life we could have made a future and looked forward to the present.

Your absence in my youth made me an angry person. You filled me with false hopes and broken promises. You missed out on the important years of my life. My education, baseball games and helping me set my goals.

I missed out on the fishing trips, the father and son talks and most of all your love and support. I didn't have that male role model there to direct and guide me.
I guess your shoes weren't large enough to carry the both of us.

Dad, I have learned a lesson from all of this. A lesson of how important it is to be involved in your children's life. When I get married and have children, I will give them everything and more of what I never received from you. Even if you didn't have the finances to provide for me, your time would have been sufficient.

Today, I want to buy you a new pair of shoes a pair large enough for the both of us. I can do this because I never forgot about you. At my games I use to always hope and pray that when I hit that home run, I would hear your voice from the crowd shouting with much pride, that's my son! I hit those home runs for you. You never saw them, you never even taught me how to pitch.

But that's ok. I may never understand why you were absent all these years from my life and because of the person that I am today and followed by the person whom I represent, "Jesus Christ", I can stand and be man enough to say. Dad, I forgive you.

Your Son.

My sincere sister in Christ

My sister, I thank God for you. You are truly a blessing.
No matter what goes on in my life you are always there.

When I am feeling lost or like giving up, you always know when and
where to find me.

God always enlightens you to deliver those encouraging, nurturing
words of comfort and peace, those words that flow from your spirit into
my ears and get delivered into my heart.

My sister, I call you sincere, you are sincerely Christ driven!
You are sincerely blessed!

God will always send confirmation through those that He knows He can
trust to deliver His word.
Those He can trust are the one's who will receive Him.

You were chosen to be the "Intercessor" that God can use to pray for His people.
"You are the one that God will pour out His blessings to".
You are the one who walks by Faith!

My sister, I thank you!

I pray that God will continue to use you mightily as His living vessel.
I pray that God will continue to anoint you with His Holy Spirit!
For you stand to be blessed!

Amen.

Marriage Enrichment

"Two joined together as one"
When God created man he fulfilled mans needs by
providing him with a helpmate,
a woman. Ordaining them to be joined together as one in
"Holy Matrimony".

To this union, you will find yourselves submitting to each other,
sharing ideas, making decisions,
as well as loving, supporting, honoring,
and respecting each other's needs for better or worse in sickness and in health.

Marriage is sacred for it's a vow made unto God.
Through this enrichment, blessings will surely come.
Only, unto death do you part.

Amen.

I'm a wonderful gift of love

I often get confused when I don't know, which way to go.
My security shattered, I'm left with know one to turn to, oh no!
Driven by many out there in the world,
Misguiding me and treating me unfair.
Where's mommy and daddy, do they no longer care.

Help! I need your guidance; I thought that I should let you know.

You know that I am an inheritance from the Mighty one above; He
blessed your womb to carry this special seed. Why can't you appreciate
this wonderful gift of love?

I know that you may be having problems, please don't take it out on me
anymore!
Get down on your knees and pray, repent and ask God for forgiveness
and please be true.

I can't continue going on this emotional roller coaster ride. I'm getting dizzy aren't you?

The Bible state that a family that prays together stay together is this where we missed our cue? Let's come together and pray at least I know God's word is true.

The Holy Spirit is a bond and a permanent securing glue. Mommy and Daddy, I love you. Please help make this dream come true.

Amen.

Off to college

From the time you were born prayers surrounded your life. You were a special gift that **God** felt a need to bring into this world.

When you where a child you would always talk about what you wanted to be and what you wanted to do when you grew up.

The time has come to let you **fly**, to establish your independence and use the knowledge that you were taught through out your life.

You will be faced with the challenges of the world, responsible for making your own decisions and with prayer, wise enough to make the right choices. It's a part of growing up. Because of whom you represent, **"Jesus Christ"**, you will be faced with temptation and when it comes your way, just look back on the principles that you were taught and you will make it through.

You will meet new friends. There will be many doors that others will try to force you to go through. Ask the **Lord** to be your guide.

It's time to adhere to the goals, dreams and accomplishments that you have set forth.

Your destination has started; you've taken another step. When you've completed your education you will come back bold, more determined, and strong willed. You will be an example for generations to come of what **God** can do.

Don't limit yourself in your ability to succeed. Always remember you have the upper hand for you have "**Jesus Christ**".

Travel your destiny. Walk in the spirit of Excellence. Reach beyond the stars. And "**Fly**".

God bless you!

We are family

When God created the family He had a plan. He created us unique, special and in the image of Him.
He created us with a purpose. He gave us hope, wisdom, knowledge and understanding.

He added a touch of, prosperity, wealth and the will to prevail.
He created us to be fruitful and to multiply.
His hope was for us to pray together and to stay together.

He created us to encourage when one is discouraged.
He blessed us with the opportunity to build relationships.
He created us to praise Him and to honor and obey Him.
He created us to love one another as He so loves us.

He blessed with us the ultimate gift of Salvation to enter into eternal life with Him through "Jesus Christ".

We are family a creation that was blessed from above.

Amen.

SECTION 7
~Going Home Celebration~

A Celebration of Remembrance

Come celebrate my going home service to be with The Lord!

Grieve if you must, but only for a short time. Your weeping may endure through the night, but joy shall come in the morning.

I know that this is a time that my presence will be missed, but you must remember that our memories will always exist.

Please don't fight over my processions even if I left them to you in my will, don't let those processions of things; separate the love that we all once shared.

Those things that I left behind were not worthy to follow me the promise land.
To a mansion so worthy, with the crafting of God's own hands. My mansion came furnished with God's unconditional Love. Furnished with rubies and diamonds and streets paved in gold.

For the battle has been won and my destination has been fulfilled. This is a journey that we all must travel. But only those who abide by God's commandments shall be in His will.

Rest assured my loved one's that my soul is at peace. Keep the peace between you my love one's and focus on God's promises, and we shall see each other again.

Amen.

Don't mourn my death celebrate my life!

Weep if you must. Let your tears be memories of joy and not tears of sorrow. In your hearts I know I'll always be remembered.

Life on earth is temporary and death is something that we all must face. My living has not been in vain. My shackles have been broken and I have earned my wings and have been blessed to fly home to glory and to spend eternity with our Lord and Savior Jesus Christ.

I have left my legacy behind as I have followed our Lords commands. This is also required of you in order for you to earn your wings, so you could fly and be blessed to spend eternity with Jesus Christ. When the time comes for you to depart this world your life will be a celebration too!

Amen.

I Have Been Set Free

The time has come to join my Heavenly Father
Jesus Christ. A time so rewarding and great!

Though my eyes may be shut and my last breath
Had been taken doesn't mean that this will be
The last time that I will see your ever loving faces.

Some of you may cry, some may rejoice
and some may be in shock, but one thing
I want you all to know is that I will forever love you.

I lived out my time on earth and have gone home
where I am now free. So, I ask that you live each day
as if it were your last because one day it shall be.

You too shall be in my place and will be blessed with
God's everlasting grace.

You too shall be free.

Amen.

Printed in the United States
by Baker & Taylor Publisher Services